THE WISDOM OF ST AUGUSTINE

THE WISDOM
OF
St AUGUSTINE

Compiled and introduced by David Winter

William B. Eerdmans Publishing Company
Grand Rapids, Michigan

This edition copyright © 1997 Lion Publishing

This edition published 1997 in the USA
through special arrangement with
Lion Publishing by
Wm. B. Eerdmans Publishing Co.
255 Jefferson Ave. S.E., Grand Rapids,
Michigan 49503

Printed in Singapore

01 00 99 98 97 7 6 5 4 3 2 1

ISBN 0-8028-3854-5

Series editor: Philip Law

Project editor: Angela Handley

Book designer: Nicholas Rous

Jacket designer: Gerald Rogers

CONTENTS

Augustine of Hippo was born in what is now Algeria in AD354. Although his mother, Monica, was a devout Christian, Augustine turned his back on the faith for the first thirty years of his life, preferring various philosophies of the time, especially a rather strange, dualistic religion called Manicheism. It was not until his time as public orator in Milan, in 386, that he first came under the spell of the golden-tongued Bishop Ambrose. After a long and agonizing struggle both with his conscience – he had a mistress and an illegitimate son – and his intellect, he finally surrendered to the claims of Christ on a hot August afternoon while reading words of St Paul from his Epistle to the Romans. He was baptized the following Easter.

Just as he was a reluctant convert, so Augustine was reluctant first to become a priest and then to be a bishop. In the latter role he became an outstanding exponent of the Christian faith, arguing its cause against secular intellectuals and various Christian heresies. His sermons were meticulously recorded in books by his followers and Augustine himself was a prolific writer, so that literally thousands of his works remain.

His great discovery, which has deeply affected the Church's understanding ever since, was over the question of 'justification'. How can sinful people be accepted by a holy God? Augustine, following closely the argument of St Paul, saw it solely as an act of God's 'grace' – an undeserved gift, to be received by faith. It was to 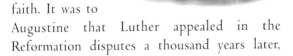 Augustine that Luther appealed in the Reformation disputes a thousand years later, even though Augustine has always been revered as a teacher of Catholic Christianity.

Here is a man who was one of the greatest thinkers in the history of the Church and yet was himself a humble and contrite follower of Jesus Christ. His words are worth hearing. They have a timeless wisdom.

Augustine wrote in Latin. There are many different translations of his works. These extracts are the compiler's own free translation. Sources are only cited for longer extracts – many of the brief sayings are available to the modern reader in compilations drawn from Augustine's sermons and writings.

DAVID WINTER

IMAGES OF GOD

A GREAT GOD AND A SMALL HEART

How can the infinite God of earth and heaven come into my small heart? And how can I invite to enter one who is already there, because he is present in all things?

Yet even heaven and earth cannot contain you, any more than my heart can. It is not possible to limit one who fills everything. But to say you are everywhere, Lord, is not to say that everywhere has all of you. Though you fill all things, you do not of necessity give them all of yourself. So I will pray that my heart, where you already have a foothold, may receive more and more of you, until one day the whole of me will be filled with the whole of you.

Confessions

THE GOD OF PARADOX

You are a God of infinite power and yet utterly
merciful. You can hide yourself from us and
yet be with us all the time. You are the creator
of both raw energy and gentle beauty. You
never change, and yet you are the author of
change everywhere. You are neither old nor
young (being eternal), yet you make all things
new. You are endlessly active and yet the source
of true rest. You love totally, but without
obsession, you possess us completely, but
without anxiety or domination. You owe us
nothing, but pay off all the debts of our sins.

Meditation on Psalm 35:10

THE BEAUTY OF THE CREATOR

The order, arrangement, beauty, change and movement of the visible world declare that it could only have been the work of God, who is indescribably and invisibly great and indescribably and invisibly beautiful.

THE HUMILITY OF CHRIST

I was not humble enough to accept the humble Jesus as my God. I didn't understand the lesson of his weakness — that the eternal 'Word', higher than everything in creation, only raises to his heights those who, like him, are prepared to be brought low. He fashioned for himself here on earth a humble dwelling from clay — sharing the 'uniform' of our bodies — through which he could bring up to his heights those who were prepared to share his depths.

Confessions

THE GROUND OF OUR BEING

As the Apostle Paul says, 'He is not far from any one of us, for in him we live and move and have our being'. Scripture also says, 'From him and through him and in him are all things'.

If everything has its being in God, then apart from him how can the living live or the moving move? So the greatest human misery is to be separated from the one without whom it is impossible to exist in a truly human way. Of course, in one sense if we exist at all we are 'in' him. But if we have no knowledge of him, no understanding, no memory of or love for him, then we cannot really be said to be 'with' him. Our minds, made in the image of his mind, are so devoid of his memory that we cannot even be reminded what it is that we have forgotten.

On the Trinity, Chapter 12

WHAT IS GOD?

God is an infinite circle whose centre
is everywhere and whose circumference
is nowhere.

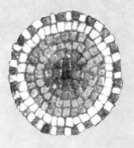

We can know what God is *not*, but mortals
cannot know what God is.

THE EYE OF FAITH

No one has ever seen God. He is real, but invisible. That means that we cannot find him with the eyes of the body, but only with the pure eyes of faith. 'Blessed are the pure in heart, for they shall see God', says the Gospel. So, if we wish to see God, let us purify the eye which alone can see him, the eye of faith.

Homily on the First Epistle of John

THE PEACE OF GOD

THE RESTLESS HEART

You have made us for yourself, and our hearts are restless till they find their rest in you.

Confessions

THE LORD WHO WATCHES OVER US

'The Lord will watch over your coming and going.' What is this 'coming' and 'going'? Surely for us it is the coming of temptation and the going of victory over it. In times of testing and temptation we need the Lord to watch over us. Indeed, he has promised that he 'will not permit us to be tempted beyond our strength'. So God watches over our coming into temptation, but he also watches over our emergence from it: 'when you are tempted, he will also provide a way'.

Not only that, but the one who watches over our coming and going never sleeps. Choose for your Protector one who never drops off! All human guardians fail in the end, but the Protector of Israel is utterly reliable, from now until the end of time.

Homily on Psalm 121

GOODNESS IS A GIFT

The mind of man is miserable and longs for happiness. It can only hope for this because change is possible, otherwise the mind could neither move from happiness to misery, nor from misery to happiness. Under the rule of an all-powerful and good God nothing but the mind's sin and his justice could have made it miserable. And nothing but the mind's goodness and the Lord's rewarding of it can make it happy. Yet even the goodness is a gift from the one whose reward is the happiness.

On the Trinity, Chapter 15

THE EAR OF GOD

At the heart of every human being is the ear
of God. Human ears hear human voices.
God's ear hears the voice of the heart.

Homily on Psalm 119

HOLDING ON TO GOD

If someone wishes for true happiness, he must hold on to what is lasting – that which no misfortune, however serious, could take away. Only God is seen to be eternal, only God remains for ever. Therefore true happiness can only be found in holding on to God.

Dialogue on 'The Happy Life'

The Meaning
of Faith

THE LIFE THAT LASTS

Any commitment of the human heart is pain, unless it be commitment to you, Lord. That is true even when we fasten on to the most beautiful things that you have made — tree, flower or bud. They hasten towards perfect beauty in the Spring, but come the Autumn they wither and die. They have no choice. It is the destiny of created things to pass away.

So it is sheer folly to invest all our affection in any creature, subject to this law of mortality. Their beauty may invoke my praise, but I must accept that they hasten towards oblivion. It is the way the world is, an endless succession of parts, each one making way for its successor.

'But do I ever depart?' asks the Word of God. He is present in all that he has made, so that we can see him in all his works and find delight in the skill of his hands. On that basis, we can indeed love what God has made, provided we recognize his presence and his power.

Not only that, but in the Son of God this cycle of mortality was broken. He came to earth to bear our death, the death of a creature. But through the life of God within him he conquered its hold. Because he lives, we too can live in him.

Confessions

HUMAN RIGHTS

I saw that no created being had any absolute right to exist of itself. Yet it has a 'right' to exist, but not its *own* right. It exists only because God exists, it is totally dependent on him. But that existence is not absolute, because a creature is not what its Creator is, eternal. So it follows that every creature has a being, because it is made by God, but no creature has an absolute being, because it is not what God is, eternal.

From this I drew a conclusion. It would be wise for me to hold fast to God, because apart from him I too, as a creature, have no absolute being. But in him I can be what he is.

Confessions

PAST, PRESENT, FUTURE

Trust the past to God's mercy, the present to God's love and the future to God's providence.

SIGHT AND FAITH

We often believe things which we have not seen and cannot visualize. We believe that our parents conceived us. We believe that we have distant ancestors. None of these things can we know by sight, deduction or reason. We simply accept them on the word of someone else. Of course, that 'someone else' must be regarded by us as reliable and trustworthy, and what they tell us must not contradict what we know to be true from other sources. So knowledge depends on things seen and things believed. Of the first we are our own witnesses. For the second, we depend on trustworthy witnesses. But that second kind of knowledge is not inferior to sight, because it is based on the evidence of those we have judged to be absolutely reliable. As the Lord himself said, 'Blessed are those who *have not seen* but have believed'.

Meditation on Matthew 5:8

THE REWARDS
OF FAITH

THE ULTIMATE PRIZE

To see God is the promised goal
of all our actions and the
promised height of all our joys.

LEARNING OF THE SPIRIT

The things of the Spirit do not come naturally
to us, like learning our mother tongue. We are
fallen, and the things of God are therefore
strange to us. Of course, interest, joy and
delight will help me learn, but behind them
there needs to be the divine compulsion, the
pressure of the Holy Spirit's firm but loving
discipline.

Confessions

THE PRIORITY OF LOVE

Love God... and then do what you like.

THE PROCESS OF RENEWAL

Spiritual renewal is not accomplished in one moment of conversion, in which our sins are forgiven. After all, it is one thing to recover from a fever, but quite another to regain one's health after it. It is one thing to remove a spear from a wound, but quite another for the wound to heal completely. So to begin the cure we remove the cause of the sickness, and this occurs through the forgiveness of our sins. Then there follows the process of healing: 'our inner man is renewed from day to day', as the Apostle said. To be thus renewed by daily progress in the knowledge, justice and holiness of God is to be converted from the temporal to the eternal and from the carnal to the spiritual. Our success in this depends entirely on God, for 'without me you can do nothing'.

On the Trinity, Chapter 17

TRUE RELIGION

True religion unites the human soul to God.
That means that it unites to him, by a process
of reconciliation, that which had been split
apart, as it were, by our sin.

THE LOVE OF GOD

ARROWS OF LOVE

'The sharp arrows of the powerful' are the words of God. When he looses them, they penetrate right into the heart. Yet they are not agents of death, like ordinary arrows, but of love and life. The Lord is skilled at firing arrows of love, and those who fire the arrows of his Word also fire arrows of love. If they strike into the heart of someone who already loves it is only to strengthen that love. And if they strike into the heart where love grows cold, it is only to fan it back into a blaze.

Meditation on Psalm 120:4

On Earth and in Heaven

Jesus said, 'No one goes up to heaven except the one who came down from heaven, the Son of Man who is in heaven'. Here is a great truth: Jesus was on earth and he was in heaven. He was on earth because he became flesh, like us. He was in heaven because he is divine. He was born of a human mother without separating himself from his heavenly Father.

It was God's purpose that he should become the 'Son of Man' and also that we should become sons of God. The one follows from the other. He came down to earth because of us; we go up to heaven because of him.

Homily on John's Gospel, Chapter 3

CHRIST'S CHOICE

He could have come down from the cross,
but he preferred to rise up from the tomb.

THE SUBTLETY
OF SIN

FOLLOWING THE CROWD

Young men don't laugh much on their own, or boast much on their own. But when they get together, what starts as fun ends up as something cruel, greedy or vicious. They're afraid of being different, of standing against the crowd, of being thought of as cowards. They are ashamed that they aren't shameless! What a travesty of human nature, that friendship and companionship, gifts of God, can be so perverted – that what is essentially good can yet seduce us into sin.

Confessions

THE GIVER AND THE GIFT

It is all too possible to want gifts from the Lord, but not the Lord himself — which seems to imply that the gift is preferable to the Giver!

TOO LATE I LOVED YOU

Too late I loved you, beauty so old yet always new! Too late I loved you! And Lo, all the while you were within me – and I, an alien to myself, searched for you elsewhere.

Confessions

THE CITY OF GOD

THE TRUE COMMONWEALTH

Where there is not that justice by which the one supreme God rules over a city obedient to his gracious will, there is not a fellowship of people united in a common sense of right and community of interest. And where that does not exist, there is not a 'people' nor is there a state, because where there is no people there is no commonwealth.

The City of God, Chapter 23

KNOWING HEAVEN NOW

The supreme mark of the City of God –
heaven – is everlasting and perfect peace.
There nothing can harm, nothing can hurt.
In comparison, even the richest life on earth
is inadequate – what can food, clothes, money,
success and fame offer that can match the
peace and joy of the Celestial City? Yet it is
possible to live in such a way on earth that we
can enjoy, if only in hope, the bliss of heaven,
and that way is to live this life for the sake of
the other one.

The City of God, Chapter 20

AN ORDERED PEACE

Peace of body and soul comes from an ordered and healthy life. Peace between human beings comes from an ordered agreement to live together. Peace between man and God comes from a faithful obedience to eternal order and law. The peace of the Celestial City is a perfectly ordered and harmonious unity of one another in the enjoyment of God. The peace of all things lies in that essential quality of order, for order ensures that everything, whether great or small, is in its proper relationship to everything else.

The City of God

Picture Acknowledgments

1: St Augustine by P. de Bounguida, 14th century, copyright © Ronald Sheridan Ancient Art and Architecture Collection.

All other illustrations supplied by Sonia Halliday as follows.

2/3, 41: Mosaic of Christ seated on throne, surrounded by angels, 6th century, S. Apollinare Nuovo, Ravenna.

4/5, 6, 12, all triangular folio decorations and all header decorations: Mosaic of pigeon, 5th century, Curium, Cyprus.

7, 18 and cover: Details from mosaic of the baptism of Christ, 5th century, baptistry of the Avians, Ravenna.

9, 15 (detail): Circular Roman mosaic, 5th century, Curium, Cyprus.

17: Detail from mosaic in cupola, 5th century, Baptistry, Ravenna.

21: Mosaic of the Good Shepherd, 5th century, Galla Placida, Ravenna.

23: Mosaic of the calling of Peter and Andrew, 6th century, S. Apollinare, Ravenna.

27: Mosaic of partridge, 3rd century, Paphos, Cyprus.

29: Detail from mosaic of the procession of the Wise Virgins, S. Apollinare Nuovo, Ravenna.

30: Detail from mosaic of man and lion, 2nd century, Cherba, Tunisia.

32: Detail from the Neptune mosaic of a man planting and a hound, 2nd century, Cherba, Tunisia.

35: Mosaic of St Mark, 6th century, S. Vitale, Ravenna.

39: Mosaic of a slave, 3rd century, Paphos, Cyprus.

43: Mosaic, 6th century, in the apse of S. Vitale, Ravenna.

47: Mosaic of guinea fowl, 5th century, Curium, Cyprus.